Letts

English BASICS

FOR AGES 10-11
KEY STAGE 2

Contents

Unstressed vowels

Look and learn

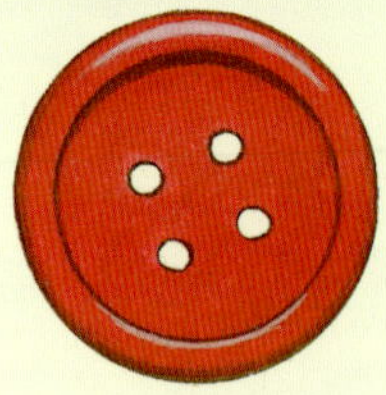

butt**o**n

cel**e**brate

Sometimes vowels in longer words are **not stressed**, or pronounced. These vowels are often difficult to hear. The words above both contain **unstressed vowels**.

Practice

Fill in the missing unstressed vowels in each word below. Use a dictionary if necessary.

1. env___lope **2.** b___s___ness

3. comp___ny **4.** entr___nce

5. ment___l **6.** photogr___pher

7. diction___ry **8.** valu___ble

9. secr___t___ry **10.** int___rest

11. cem___t___ry **12.** trav___l

Challenge

Join up the syllables.

dif	nes	y
Wed	ar	ture
his	fer	day
bach	na	ate
sep	el	ent
sig	tor	or

Write the word and underline any unstressed vowels.

1. ________
2. ________
3. ________
4. ________
5. diff<u>e</u>r<u>e</u>nt
6. ________

Root words

Look and learn

A **root word** is a word to which **prefixes** or **suffixes** may be added.
Sometimes the root word is **easy** to see. Sometimes the root word is **harder** to work out.

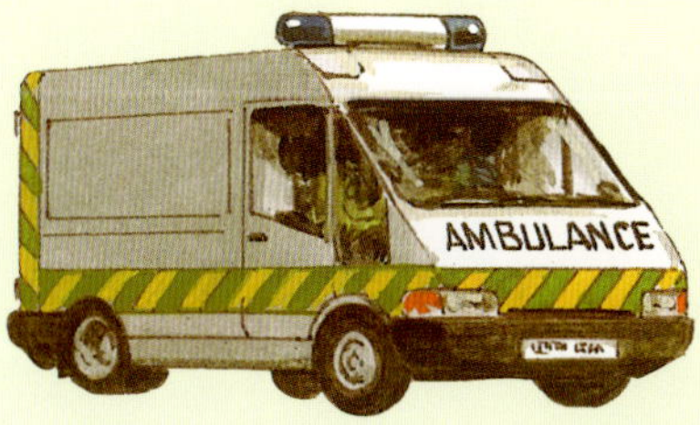

unhelpful (root word – help)

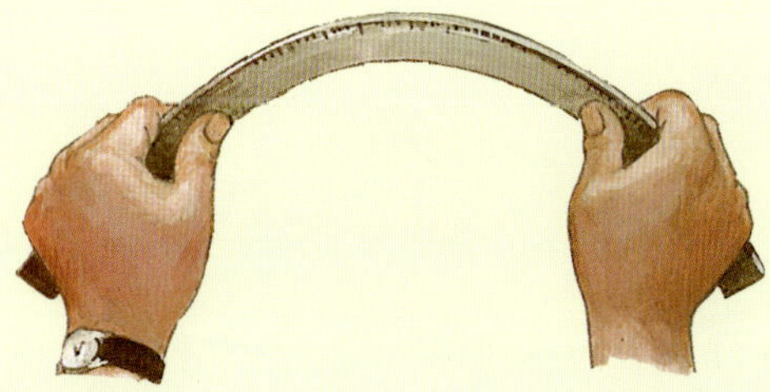

flexibility (root word – flexible)

Practice

Find and write the root word of each longer word below.

1. bicycle	cycle	**2.** triangle	angle
3. exported	port	**4.** injustice	Justice
5. friendliness	friend	**6.** uncontrollable	Controll
7. admission	mission	**8.** magically	magic
9. disagreement	disagree	**10.** signature	sighn
11. competition	~~pe~~ compete	**12.** proposal	propose
13. generously generouse	~~generouse~~		
14. unsuitable	sui~~table~~		
15. sympathise	sympathy		

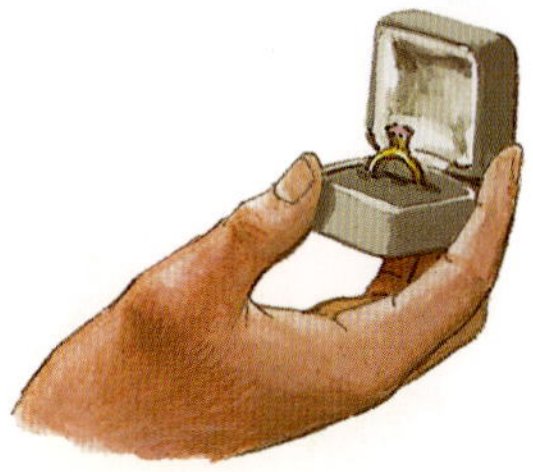

Challenge

Add prefixes and suffixes. Make at least two longer words from each root word.

root word	longer words
appear	disappear, appearing
cover	Covering, uncover
like	likeadle, dislike
comfort	Comftible, uncomftible
colour	colorfull, Coloring
weak	weaker, weakness

Dashes and brackets

Look and learn

A **dash** holds words apart. It is stronger than a comma. It is not as strong as a full stop.

Brackets enclose information to show it is separate from the rest of the sentence.

Sam ordered his favourite meal – curry.

The Pyramids (found in Egypt) are huge.

Practice

Choose the best ending to complete each sentence.

1. There is only one sport worth playing – football!
2. My sister loves pop music – __________
3. John Logie Baird invented television – __________
4. I have got a mountain bike – __________
5. One girl was different – __________
6. I read a great book last week – __________
7. Get your homework in on time – __________
8. Tom won a competition – __________
9. The monster appeared – __________
10. In the attic I found an old friend – __________

Sentence endings
a marvellous invention.
or you'll be in trouble.
she had pink hair.
all green and slimy.
football!
my old teddy.
Treasure Island.
I hate it!
for painting a picture.
a silver one.

Challenge

Choose the best "filling" to go inside each pair of brackets.

over 26 miles	a red sports car	in Africa	a famous composer	1666

1. The Great Fire of London (__________) was terrible.
2. Mount Kilimanjaro (__________) always has snow at the top.
3. Beethoven (__________) wrote lots of music.
4. Each year there is a marathon (__________) in New York.
5. The man parked his car (__________).

Parts of speech

Look and learn

Words may be divided into groups called **parts of speech**. Three important parts of speech are: **nouns**, **verbs** and **adjectives**.

This is a **noun**. It is a **naming word**.

The happy lady was laughing.

This is an **adjective**. It is a **describing word**. It tells us more about the **noun**.

This is a **verb**. It is a word that describes **actions**.

Practice

In the following sentences:
circle the adjectives; tick the nouns; underline the verbs.

1. I tripped over the uneven floor.
2. The silly boy crashed his new bike.
3. When the old lady reached her house, she sat down.
4. We saw wild horses in the forest.
5. The large crowd cheered as the skilful player scored.
6. The giggling girls annoyed the teacher.
7. A prickly hedgehog snuffled in the dry leaves.
8. The lazy man was sleeping under the tall tree.

Challenge

Think of a suitable word for each gap. In the brackets write if it is a noun, verb or adjective.

1. Sam put the ______________ suitcase on the floor. (______________)
2. Athens is the capital of ______________. (______________)
3. The mountaineers ______________ to the summit. (______________)
4. The children sang loudly at the ______________. (______________)
5. The cat's ______________ was soft and silky. (______________)
6. The helicopter ______________ over the motorway. (______________)

Look and learn

We sometimes join two **clauses** together by using a **connective**.

Sam is good at swimming (clause 1) because (connective) he practises a lot. (clause 2)

Practice

Choose the best connective to join each pair of sentences.

		Connectives
1.	I turned on the tap ___so that___ I could have a drink.	(so that/as)
2.	The helicopter flew near the volcano ______________ it erupted.	(where/when)
3.	I know a man ______________ has seven cats.	(which/who)
4.	I visit my grandmother ______________ I have time.	(that/whenever)
5.	Anna stopped blowing up the balloon ______________ it burst.	(so/in case)
6.	Tom pumped up his tyre ______________ he wouldn't get a puncture.	(until/so that)
7.	The Middle East is important ______________ it has lots of oil.	(during/as)
8.	I always do my homework ______________ I watch TV.	(although/before)
9.	The children were running ______________ they were late.	(if/because)
10.	The cat chased the mouse ______________ it came out of the hole.	(since/when)

Challenge

Think of a good clause to complete each sentence.

1. I ran until ______________________________.

2. The children quietened down when ______________________________.

3. Alice found a key that ______________________________.

4. Tom fell off the wall on which ______________________________.

5. Lucy was a girl who ______________________________.

Prefixes and suffixes

Look and learn

We add **prefixes** and **suffixes** to words to **change their meanings**.

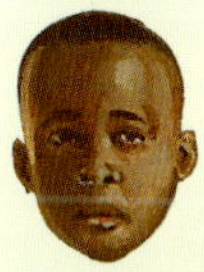

happy – **un**happy

A **prefix** is added to the **beginning** of a word. It **does not** change the spelling of the root word.

empty – empti**ness**

A **suffix** is added to the **end** of a word. It may **sometimes** change the spelling of the root word.

Practice

Choose the correct prefix to complete each word.

1. _bi_ cycle (con/bi) **2.** ____ merge (sub/tele) **3.** ____ plane (in/aero)

4. ____ mature (in/im) **5.** ____ considerate (in/im) **6.** ____ responsible (ex/ir)

7. ____ angle (tri/micro) **8.** ____ legal (ex/il) **9.** ____ fix (pre/de)

10. ____ face (mis/de) **11.** ____ understand (dis/mis) **12.** ____ fill (dis/re)

13. ____ metre (centi/aqua) **14.** ____ clockwise (anti/mal) **15.** ____ change (for/ex)

Challenge

Take the suffix off each word. Write the root word.

1. babies _baby_ **2.** nastiness ________

3. beautiful ________ **4.** quarrelling ________

5. shiny ________ **6.** operation ________

7. knives ________ **8.** microscopic ________

9. burglar ________ **10.** mysterious ________

11. attendance ________ **12.** excitable ________

Active and passive verbs

Look and learn

The thief **stole** the jewels.

A verb is **active** when the subject of the sentence does the action.

The jewels **were stolen** by the thief.

A verb is **passive** when the subject of the sentence has the action done to it.

Practice

Underline the verb in the each sentence. Say if it is active (A) or passive (P).

1. The lion chased the deer. (A)

2. The car was driven by the lady. (__)

3. The author wrote lots of books. (__)

4. The doctor listened to my heart. (__)

5. The cup was won by the girls. (__)

6. The tree was chopped down by the man. (__)

7. The river ran through the valley. (__)

8. The candle was blown out by the wind. (__)

9. The child bought some sweets. (__)

10. The avalanche crashed down the mountain. (__)

11. The goal was scored by Jess. (__)

12. The dog chased the cat. (__)

Challenge

Rewrite each sentence. Change the verb from passive to active.

1. The car was stopped by the police officer. The police officer stopped the car.

2. My luggage was carried by a porter. __________

3. The mouse was chased by the cat. __________

4. The gold medal was won by the relay team. __________

5. The coin was picked up by the boy. __________

6. The window was broken by the girl. __________

7. The glass was dropped by Sam. __________

8. The carrot was eaten by the horse. __________

9. All the keys were stolen by the thief. __________

10. Ben was hugged by his aunt. __________

Where do our words come from?

Look and learn

English is not just **one language**. It is made up of words taken from many **other languages**.

spaghetti

Italy

jungle

India

ballet

France

yacht

Holland

Practice

Fill in each gap with a word from the Word Box.

Here are some words that come from France.

Word Box	
duvet	banquet
ballet	buffet
bracket	cabaret
trumpet	sachet
scarlet	ricochet
bouquet	blanket

1. Scarlet is a dark red colour.
2. A ______________ holds up a shelf.
3. A ______________ is a bunch of flowers.
4. A ______________ is a small packet.
5. A ______________ is a musical instrument.
6. A ______________ is a bed covering, filled with feathers.
7. A ______________ is a number of different acts.
8. ______________ is a kind of dance.
9. A ______________ is a special feast.
10. A ______________ is a bed covering.
11. A ______________ is a meal where you serve yourself.
12. A ______________ is when something hits a surface and bounces off.

Challenge

Use a dictionary to help you. Decide which country each word comes from.

Word	Country of origin
1. pizza	
2. schooner	
3. café	
4. kangaroo	
5. wok	
6. moccasins	
7. bungalow	
8. reggae	

There is a word from each of these countries: France, America, Jamaica, China, Italy, India, Australia, Holland.

Mnemonics

Look and learn

A **mnemonic** is a way of remembering the spelling of tricky words.

An island **is land** surrounded by water.

Practice

Which words do these clues help you to solve?

favourite
piece
believe
business
weight
young
bicycle
miserable
separate
conscience

1. Catch a **bus in** to your ___business___.
2. ______________ has a **rat in** it.
3. ______________ is **our** best word.
4. Don't ride your ______________ in **icy** weather.
5. ______________ has **science** in it.
6. I would like a ______________ of **pie**.
7. **You** are only ______________ once.
8. Never ______________ a **lie**.
9. A **miser** is always ______________.
10. What's the ______________ of **eight** people?

Challenge

Underline the tricky bit in each word.
Make up your own mnemonic to help you spell each word.

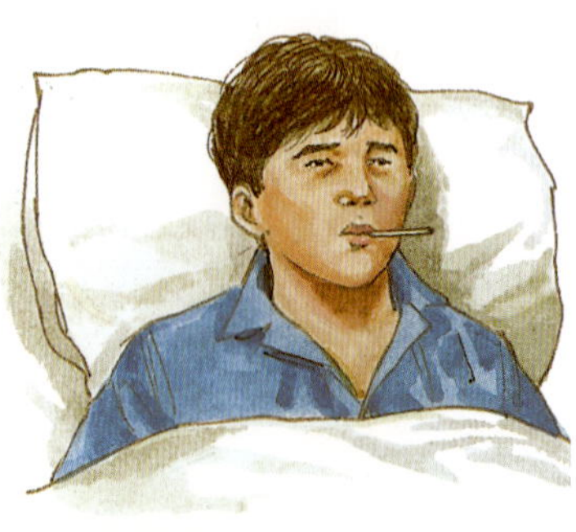

1. temperature ______________________________
2. skeleton ______________________________
3. vegetable ______________________________
4. cupboard ______________________________
5. sword ______________________________
6. restaurant ______________________________
7. marriage ______________________________
8. headache ______________________________
9. friend ______________________________
10. chocolate ______________________________

Punctuation

Look and learn

Punctuation helps us to make sense of what we read. **Punctuation marks** make writing easier for us to understand. They can make a lot of difference!

The soldier entered on his head, a helmet on each foot, a sandal in his hand. He had his trusty sword. ✗

The soldier entered. On his head a helmet, on each foot a sandal. In his hand he had his trusty sword. ✓

Practice

Rewrite each sentence. Punctuate it correctly.

1. the man asked is it raining ____________________
2. Ive lost my pen rohan shouted ____________________
3. the burglar whispered someones coming ____________________
4. wheres my bag mrs shah asked ____________________
5. you will need a pen a ruler and some paper ____________________
6. the noise a loud banging noise was awful ____________________
7. the childrens clothes were on the floor ____________________
8. what a lovely surprise the teacher said ____________________
9. pass the salt please sams dad asked ____________________
10. the boys coat was torn ____________________

Challenge

Rewrite this sign. Make it mean the opposite by changing only the puntuation marks.

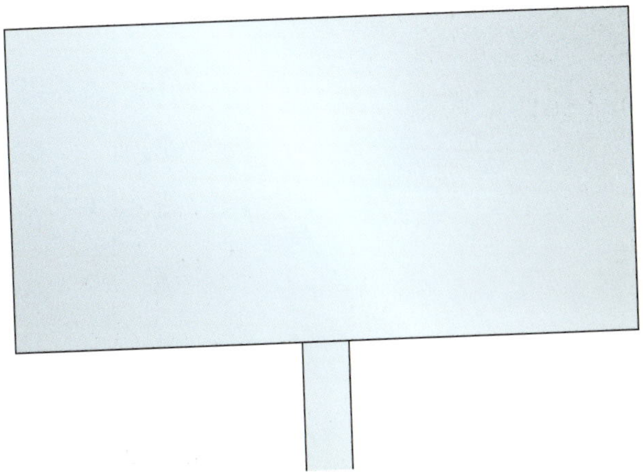

Word origins

Look and learn

The English language has been influenced by **many other languages**. Understanding the **origins** of words sometimes helps us spell them.

From the word 'signum' we get the words 'signal' and 'signature'.

Practice

Complete the chart correctly with words from the Word Box.

	Latin word	Meaning	English words
1.	signum	a sign	signal, signature
2.	scribere	to write	
3.	videre	to see	
4.	pedum	foot	
5.	gratus	pleasing	
6.	specare	to look	
7.	liber	free	
8.	civis	citizen	

Word Box	
describe	pedal
congratulate	vision
spectator	signal
evident	liberty
liberal	grateful
signature	city
civilian	pedestrian
spectacles	scribble

Challenge

Complete the chart with some words you think might come from these Greek words:

	Greek word	Meaning	English words
1.	phone	sound	telephone, microphone
2.	geo	earth	
3.	auto	self	
4.	graph	to write	
5.	aster	a star	
6.	scope	I see	

Complex sentences

Look and learn

Alice found a key which opened the door.

main clause | subordinate clause

Many complex sentences are made up of a **main clause** and a **subordinate clause** (a less important clause).

Practice

Join up each main clause from Set A with an appropriate subordinate clause from Set B.

Set A	Set B
1. The children began to shout	when I went to bed.
2. Last night I read a good book	which is in Greece.
3. Alexander Bell was the inventor	because they are so colourful.
4. I visited Athens	when the teacher left the room.
5. I collect stamps	when the Great Fire spread in 1666.
6. Samuel Pepys lived in London	who invented the telephone.

Write the sentences you have made:

1. ______________________

2. ______________________

3. ______________________

4. ______________________

5. ______________________

6. ______________________

Challenge

Think of a suitable subordinate clause to finish each complex sentence:

1. I like cats because ______________________.

2. My pet rabbit escaped when ______________________.

3. I climbed the tree so that ______________________.

4. I saw the queen when ______________________.

5. The explorer kept walking until ______________________.

6. The snake slithered through the grass just as ______________________.

Look and learn

Look before you leap.

A proverb is a **wise saying** that has been around a **long time**.

Practice

Choose the best word to complete each proverb.

never	clean	worm	cooks	one
nine	speed	well	birds	served

1. Too many ___cooks___ spoil the broth.
2. More haste, less ____________.
3. First come, first ____________.
4. Better late than ____________.
5. If a job is worth doing, it's worth doing ____________.
6. New brooms sweep ____________.
7. A stitch in time saves ____________.
8. Two heads are better than ____________.
9. The early bird catches the ____________.
10. ____________ of a feather flock together.

Challenge

Finish each of these proverbs:

1. Every cloud ________________________________.
2. Empty vessels ________________________________.
3. Don't put all your eggs ________________________________.
4. Still waters ________________________________.
5. One good turn ________________________________.
6. A rolling stone ________________________________.
7. Great minds ________________________________.
8. Out of the frying pan ________________________________.

Syllables

Look and learn

par – a – chute (3 syllables)

Words can be broken down into smaller parts, called **syllables**.

Practice

Work out these syllable 'sums'.

1. de + ter + mine = determine

2. um + brel + la = ______

3. con + fid + ent = ______

4. e + lec + tric = ______

5. in + fec + ted = ______

6. in + tro + duce = ______

7. chat + ter + box = ______

8. hos + pit + al = ______

9. rest + less + ness = ______

10. re + mem + ber = ______

11. dif + fer + ent = ______

12. Jan + u + ar + y = ______

13. at + ten + tion = ______

14. u + ni + form = ______

15. con + duc + tor = ______

Challenge

Think of a suitable second syllable for each word. Then write the whole word.

1. ac + ro + bat = acrobat

2. Nov + ______ + ber = ______

3. pro + ______ + al = ______

4. help + ______ + ly = ______

5. ad + ______ + ture = ______

6. lem + ______ + ade = ______

7. ex + ______ + lent = ______

8. dis + ______ + er = ______

9. con + ______ + ent = ______

10. ex + ______ + sive = ______

Using dictionaries

Look and learn

lubricate
to oil or grease the moving parts of a machine so they run smoothly.

You can use a dictionary to find the **meaning** of a word and to check its **spelling**.

Practice

Use a dictionary to help you solve these clues. They are in alphabetical order.

1. A crobat Someone who does balancing tricks.
2. B________ Lovely – very pretty.
3. C________ Stops wine coming out of a bottle.
4. D________ Not safe – risky.
5. E________ Costs a lot.
6. F________ A shallow river crossing.
7. G________ A quick look.
8. H________ A six-sided shape.
9. I________ A pointed stick of ice.
10. J________ Make fun of person in rude way.
11. K________ A sharp cutting tool.
12. L________ A long spear carried by knights.
13. M________ Something worn over the face.
14. N________ Not wide.
15. O________ A sea creature with tentacles.
16. P________ Quiet and calm.
17. Q________ Where ships moor.
18. R________ Not long ago.
19. S________ Rare.
20. T________ A shop assistant puts money in it.
21. U________ To join together.
22. V________ Not clear.
23. W________ Clever and amusing.
24. X________ A short form of Christmas.
25. Y________ A type of sailing boat.
26. Z________ To move or climb suddenly.

Challenge

Spell these words correctly. Use a dictionary to help.

1. calender ____calendar____
2. resevoir ________
3. parliment ________
4. goverment ________
5. delicous ________
6. dissappear ________
7. somersalt ________
8. alltogether ________
9. sissors ________
10. kangeroo ________

Spelling rules

Look and learn

Some **spelling rules** are helpful to remember. One of the more commonly quoted rules is:

i (when it makes the sound **ee**) before **e** except after **c**

I bel**ie**ve the th**ie**f stole a p**ie**ce of cake.

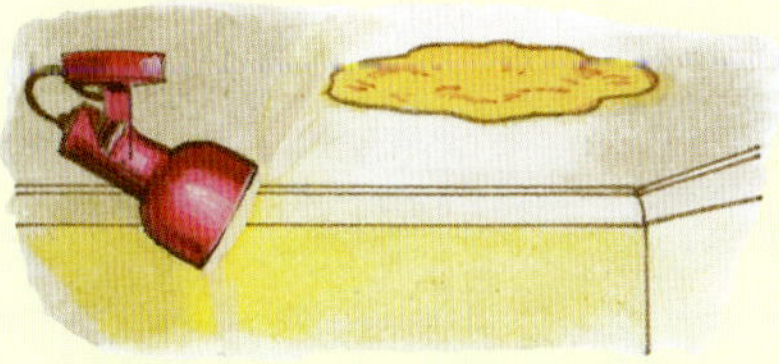

The pancake is on the c**ei**ling!

Practice

Make these words.

ie

1. ach___ve achieve **2.** bel___ve **3.** br___f **4.** ch___f **5.** f___ld

ie

6. sh___ld **7.** p___ce **8.** s___ge **9.** bab___s **10.** cop___s

ei

11. c___ling **12.** rec___ve **13.** dec___ve **14.** perc___ve **15.** conc___t

Challenge

Follow the rule! Choose **ie** or **ei**. Check in a dictionary if you are not sure.

1. pr___st **2.** misch___f

3. dec___t **4.** rel___f

5. c___ling **6.** n___ce

7. shr___k **8.** s___ve

9. conc___ted **10.** y___ld

11. rec___ve **12.** f___rce

NB: There are some words which don't stick to the rules!

seize

weird

forfeit

Conditionals

Look and learn

A **conditional verb** tells you the action **might** happen (or might have happened), because it **depends** on someone or something else.

I **would** go out if it stopped raining.

I **could** not eat the apple because it was bad.

Practice

Match up the beginnings and endings of these sentences. Circle the conditional verb in each.

1. If the snow continues
2. If you are thirsty
3. If I had the money
4. I could have swum across the river
5. I might win the jackpot
6. She would have passed the test
7. The teacher would not let us go home
8. I told you if you shouted
9. If I were the Prime Minister
10. If cows had wings

- you should have a drink.
- if I keep putting money in this machine.
- I would cut everyone's taxes.
- we might get cut off.
- until we had finished our work.
- but there were too many crocodiles.
- they would be able to fly!
- I would buy a new pair of trainers.
- you would wake the baby.
- but she didn't practise enough.

Challenge

Complete the conditional sentences with suitable endings.

1. I would like ______________________________.
2. Would you ______________________________.
3. If she pushes me again ______________________________.
4. If I win the Lottery ______________________________.
5. I might go to the party if ______________________________.
6. If only I had worked harder ______________________________.
7. If I had not overslept ______________________________.
8. No one would notice if ______________________________.

Shortening sentences

Look and learn

We can **shorten** sentences by taking out adjectives and adverbs (describing words).

The ~~tired~~ ~~old~~ man ~~slowly~~ sat down.
The man sat down.

When we write **notes** we only write down **essential** words.

This actually means:
I have put your dinner in the oven to keep it hot.

Practice

Shorten these sentences. Cross out the adjectives and adverbs.

1. The ~~small~~, ~~black~~ dog ~~noisily~~ barked at the ~~tall~~ man.
2. The pink-haired lady shouted angrily at the young waiter.
3. The fat, bearded man easily lifted his heavy sack.
4. My favourite footballer skilfully scored a beautiful goal.
5. Whizzo, the jolly clown, fell awkwardly off the stepladder.
6. Gary Goldberg, the famous singer, silently slipped out of the back door.
7. Our new car was badly damaged in the accident.
8. The chattering monkeys noisily climbed up the swaying tree.
9. The glamorous lady waited eagerly for her handsome husband.
10. My best friend quickly answered the door.

Challenge

Convert these notes into proper sentences, punctuated correctly.

Jaguars like water — good swimmers — live near rivers — catch turtles and fish — female jaguars teach young — stay with mothers for two years.

Our changing language

Look and learn

Many **words** and **expressions** have **changed**.

The **astronauts** prepared for **countdown**.

New words enter our language all the time.

Practice

Match up the old and new version of the words and phrases.

	Old	New
1.	wilt	lives
2.	saith	truly
3.	abides	will
4.	ye	look at
5.	verily	says
6.	wondrous	are
7.	behold	wonderful
8.	art	you

	Old	New
9.	over yonder	Do as you are told.
10.	hither and thither	What do you want?
11.	Do as thou art bidden.	Who lives here?
12.	to tarry awhile	over there
13.	What dost thou desire?	Are you a friend or an enemy?
14.	Art thou friend or foe?	Come here.
15.	Who abides within?	to stay for a while
16.	Come nigh.	here and there

Challenge

Tick which of these words you think have entered our language in the last 50 years.

mobile phone ✓	pen	television
farm	computer	satellite
wheelie	house	video
calculator	dinosaur	cheeseburger
mill	sneaker	trainers
floppy disk	chimney	motel
wood	Internet	astronaut

Formal language

Look and learn

We speak to each other **informally**.

You are forbidden to engage in conversation.

Official language is very **formal**.

Practice

Match up these formal and informal ways of saying things.

Formal	Informal
1. Can you decipher my writing?	Thanks for the gift.
2. Kindly append your signature.	Please answer my letter.
3. Many thanks for your donation.	Keep off the grass.
4. I regret I am unable to attend.	Get out of my way.
5. Please reply to my correspondence.	Can you read my writing?
6. I bid you farewell.	Pay up at once.
7. Please desist from walking on the grass.	Sorry I can't come.
8. Apologies for any inconvenience caused.	Cheerio.
9. Do not hinder my progress.	Sorry to have bothered you.
10. Kindly settle your debt immediately.	Please sign this.

Challenge

Write what you think these formal notices mean.

1. Thieves will be prosecuted.

2. Vehicular travel prohibited.

3. You are requested not to consume your food on these premises.

4. Concealing information is a punishable offence.

5. Kindly register on entry.

6. The management cannot accept any liability for theft.

Look and learn

We can often change a **root word** by adding a **prefix**.

We can often change a **root word** by adding a **suffix**.

nonsense ← sense → sensible

(root word + prefix) (root word) (root word + suffix)

Practice

Choose a prefix from the box to complete each word.

mis	out	dis	extra
for	hemi	mid	trans
post	retro	under	
be	sub	with	sur

1. mid air
2. ______ stand
3. ______ cast
4. ______ current
5. ______ friend
6. ______ behave
7. ______ code
8. ______ face
9. ______ grade
10. ______ approve
11. ______ bid
12. ______ sphere
13. ______ plant
14. ______ ordinary
15. ______ marine

Challenge

Take the suffix off each word. Write the root word correctly.

1. historian history
2. beggar ______
3. observatory ______
4. reception ______
5. president ______
6. kingdom ______
7. argument ______
8. cowardice ______
9. magnetism ______
10. friendship ______
11. apologise ______
12. sparkle ______
13. simplify ______
14. cyclist ______

More about complex sentences

Look and learn

The chips were cold when I ate them.

main clause | subordinate clause

A **complex** sentence contains a **main clause** and a **subordinate** (less important) **clause**. The subordinate clause may not make sense on its own.

Practice

Circle the main clause and underline the subordinate clause in each sentence.

1. The wind was so cold that I put on a coat.
2. The dog dug a hole for his bone so he could bury it.
3. When I am eighteen, I am allowed to vote.
4. Until I look, I don't know what the time is.
5. Tidy up your bedroom before you get into trouble.
6. Unless you look in the cupboard, you will never find your present.
7. While the fire engines were on the way, the house burnt down.
8. Whenever I can, I go to watch Manchester United play football.
9. It often rains in November so I carry an umbrella.
10. You cannot have any sweets until you wash up.

Challenge

Complete these complex sentences by adding a subordinate clause of your own.

1. P.C. Jolly arrested the man who ____________________.
2. Anna bought a magazine which ____________________.
3. I found the treasure which ____________________.
4. Mr Desai was a teacher who ____________________.
5. Tom did not get up even though ____________________.
6. We saw many new clothes shops when ____________________.
7. Mrs Smith thanked me for ____________________.
8. The dog went to sleep after ____________________.

Phrases and clauses

Look and learn

Shireen slipped over in a muddy puddle.

clause — "Shireen slipped over"

phrase — "in a muddy puddle."

A **clause** may be used either as a **whole sentence** or as a **part of a sentence**.
A clause always contains a **verb**.

A **phrase** does **not** contain a **verb**.
A phrase does **not make sense** on its own.

Practice

Choose a phrase from the phrase box to complete each sentence.

1. The baby chicks followed behind the hen ____________.
2. The lion pounced, ____________.
3. The man carried a bag, ____________.
4. ____________, it rained hard.
5. Tom did his spellings ____________.
6. The alien spacecraft landed ____________.
7. ____________ I felt a lot better.
8. The children looked up at the ____________ clouds.
9. ____________ we go on holiday.
10. ____________ I managed to lift the heavy rock.

Phrase Box

full of dirty washing
carelessly and untidily
After my medicine
Every summer
behind the hen
With great effort
dark, rainy
quick as a flash
During the night
on the playground

Challenge

Write if each of these is a phrase (P) or a clause (C).

1. The balloons popped. (C)
2. after the party (__)
3. long and loud (__)
4. They moved quietly. (__)
5. with a sigh (__)
6. as flat as a pancake (__)
7. We skipped. (__)
8. It rained heavily. (__)
9. thunder and lightning (__)
10. before breakfast (__)
11. in a while (__)
12. The wind roared. (__)

More punctuation

Look and learn

It is important to check that your punctuation is correct!

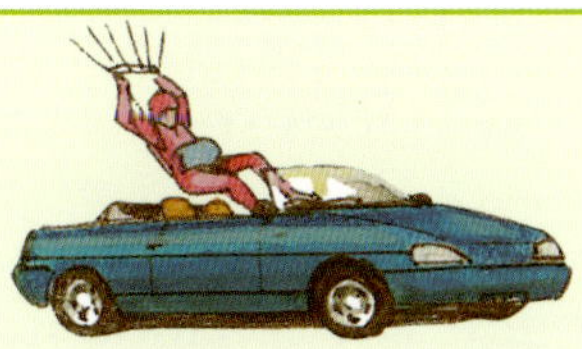

The pilot landed in his car. He drove home.

The pilot landed. In his car, he drove home.

Practice

Tick (✓) the sentences that are correctly punctuated. Cross (✗) those that are wrong.

1. After a while the car, an old wreck, rattled by. ☐
2. The boy shouted, “Please help!” ☐
3. I’m glad you came; it’s been a long time. ☐
4. Leroys’ pencil was broken ☐
5. Mrs Jones asked where is my bag? ☐
6. At the bottom of the sign it said: “No entry”. ☐
7. The Great Plague (1665) was followed by the Great Fire (1666). ☐
8. The monster shook it’s head. ☐
9. “They’re not ripe yet, the gardener explained. ☐
10. The winning numbers were: 7, 42, 47 and 50. ☐
11. The boy’s bikes had been stolen when they returned. ☐
12. The plane its engine in flames began to head towards the mountain. ☐

Challenge

Rewrite this passage. Punctuate it correctly.

marc and shireen decided to climb mount kilimanjaro after a while they stopped what a marvellous view exclaimed shireen as they progressed further marcs foot slipped he almost fell its too dangerous for me he said Im going down again

Another spelling rule

Look and learn

admi**t**

No admittance unless accompanied by an adult

admi**tt**ance

Note – We always double the **l** in words regardless of stress e.g. marvel – marvellous, travel – travelling

When a word has one vowel before a single final consonant, double the consonant before adding a suffix – if the last syllable is stressed.

Practice

Complete this chart.

	verb	+ ing	+ ed
1.	regret	regretting	regretted
2.	occur		
3.	transmit		
4.	prefer		
5.	omit		
6.	fulfil		
7.	travel		
8.	control		
9.	cancel		
10.	quarrel		

Challenge

Choose the correct form of the word to complete each sentence.

1. Let's begin at the beginning. (begin)
2. He ____________ to give me my change. (omit)
3. I am already ____________ what I said. (regret)
4. The marooned pirates were ____________ for help. (signal)
5. Our teacher is a very ____________ person. (forbid)
6. We listened to the radio ____________. (transmit)
7. The tin was wrongly ____________. (label)
8. It never ____________ to me to ask. (occur)
9. ____________ is restricted to ticket holders. (admit)
10. The naughty child was un____________. (control)

Long and short vowels

Look and learn

wĭnd

Short vowels make the **sound** of the letter.

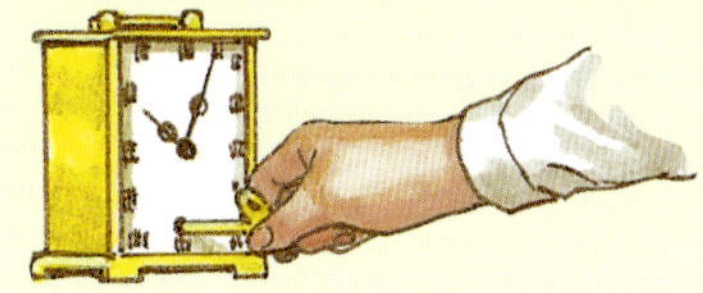

wīnd

Long vowels say the **name** of the letter.

Practice

Show whether the vowels in these words are long ¯ or short ˘.

1. blīnd **2.** stretch **3.** ghost **4.** child

5. clutch **6.** catch **7.** rabbit **8.** robot

9. comb **10.** knight **11.** halo **12.** evil

13. rubbish **14.** dentist **15.** crazy **16.** duet

17. chaos **18.** splendid **19.** tulip **20.** volcano

Challenge

1. Add **le** to the end of each word. Take care. The spelling of some root words will change.

a) table____ **b)** nibble____ **c)** rip____

d) bib____ **e)** stab____ **f)** hob____

g) wig____ **h)** snug____ **i)** tit____

j) cab____ **k)** sad____ **l)** rat____

m) net____ **n)** bug____ **o)** lad____

2. Use the words you made to complete the chart.

Words containing short vowel in first syllable.	Words containing long vowel in first syllable.
nibble	table

Common word endings

Look and learn

There is a rum**our** that a creat**ure** lives in the lake.

It is helpful to learn the spelling of common word endings.

Practice

Choose either **our** or **ure** to complete each word.

1. nat ure	**2.** flav____	**3.** fail____	**4.** hum____
5. rum____	**6.** temperat____	**7.** neighb____	**8.** fig____
9. harb____	**10.** treas____	**11.** fut____	**12.** vig____
13. inj____	**14.** glam____	**15.** splend____	**16.** pleas____
17. vap____	**18.** advent____	**19.** mixt____	**20.** hon____

Challenge

Use some of the words you made to complete these definitions.

1. Rumour Something passed around as news – but may not be true.

2. ____________ Strength. Energy.

3. ____________ To harm oneself.

4. ____________ The inability to do something.

5. ____________ The taste of something.

6. ____________ The time ahead.

7. ____________ Steam or mist.

8. ____________ Someone who lives nearby.

9. ____________ A sense of fun.

10. ____________ Something that has been mixed.

11. ____________ Something that pleases.

12. ____________ A place where ships dock.

More common word endings

Look and learn

machin**ery**

fact**ory**

libr**ary**

It is helpful to learn the spelling of common word endings.

Practice

Choose either **ery**, **ory** or **ary** to complete each word.

1. nurs_ery_ **2.** laborat____ **3.** gran____

4. fact____ **5.** diction____ **6.** discov____

7. conservat____ **8.** milit____ **9.** brew____

10. dormit____ **11.** libr____ **12.** estu____

13. refect____ **14.** bak____ **15.** scen____

16. deliv____ **17.** direct____ **18.** di____

19. mock____ **20.** jewell____

Challenge

Sort the words you made into sets. Add two more words to each set.

ery words	**ory** words	**ary** words

Similes

Look and learn

A **simile** is when one thing is compared to another using the words **as** or **like**.

My tyre was **as** flat **as** a pancake.

When my mum cleans up she's **like** a whirlwind.

Practice

Match up the beginnings and endings of these common similes.

1. as tough as	mouse
2. as blind as a	cucumber
3. as quiet as a	grass
4. as busy as a	leather
5. as green as	elephant
6. as smooth as	feather
7. as cool as a	bat
8. as brave as a	silk
9. as light as a	lion
10. as heavy as an	bee

Challenge

Make up some similes of your own to finish these sentences.

1. On a stormy day the wind is like ______________________.

2. When Tom is happy he is like ______________________.

3. When Sita gets angry she is like ______________________.

4. The hot sun was like ______________________.

5. The motorbike roared past like ______________________.

6. When I went on the Big Dipper it felt like ______________________.

7. The candyfloss tasted like ______________________.

8. The monster hissed like ______________________.

Look and learn

We can learn a lot by playing **word games**. They can help us with spelling and help **improve our vocabulary**.

Practice

Use a dictionary to help you solve this puzzle.

	Clue	Grid
1.	a bubbly drink	c h a m p a g n e
2.	a very prickly desert plant	c a _ _ _ _
3.	to hold fast to	c l _ _ _ _
4.	one hundred years	c e _ _ _ _ _
5.	to get in touch with	c o _ _ _ _ _
6.	a spice used to flavour food	c i _ _ _ _ _ _
7.	a young swan	c y _ _ _ _
8.	to bend low	c r _ _ _ _
9.	a smooth bend	c u _ _ _
10.	a hot, spicy meal	c u _ _ _

Challenge

Match up the pairs of letters in the box with the letters below to form the names of creatures.

1. heron **2.** ____mmoth **3.** ____nx

4. ____libut **5.** ____zzard **6.** ____oat

7. ____ail **8.** ____lchard **9.** ____strel

10. ____lmon **11.** ____eetah **12.** ____out

he	st	qu	ke	sa	ly
tr	ch	pi	bu	ha	ma

Answers

Page 2
Practice: 1. envelope, 2. business, 3. company, 4. entrance, 5. mental, 6. photographer, 7. dictionary, 8. valuable, 9. secretary, 10. interest, 11. cemetery, 12. travel
Challenge: 1. history, 2. signature, 3. Wednesday, 4. separate, 6. bachelor

Page 3
Practice: 2. angle, 3. port, 4. just, 5. friend, 6. control, 7. admit, 8. magic, 9. agree, 10. sign, 11. compete, 12. propose, 13. generous, 14. suit, 15. sympathy
Challenge: answers may vary

Page 4
Practice: 1. football! 2. I hate it! 3. a marvellous invention. 4. a silver one. 5. she had pink hair. 6. Treasure Island. 7. or you'll be in trouble. 8. for painting a picture. 9. all green and slimy. 10. my old teddy.
Challenge: 1. 1666, 2. in Africa, 3. a famous composer, 4. over 26 miles, 5. a red sports car

Page 5
Practice:
1. tripped (verb), uneven (adjective), floor (noun)
2. silly, new (adjectives), boy, bike (nouns), crashed (verb)
3. old (adjective), lady, house (nouns), reached, sat (verb)
4. saw (verb), wild (adjective), horses, forest (nouns)
5. large, skilful (adjectives), cheered, scored (verbs), crowd, player (nouns)
6. giggling (adjective), girls, teacher (nouns), annoyed (verb)
7. prickly, dry (adjectives), hedgehog, leaves (nouns), snuffled (verb)
8. lazy, tall (adjectives), man, tree (nouns), was sleeping (verb)

Challenge: answers may vary

Page 6
Practice: 1. so that, 2. when, 3. who, 4. whenever, 5. in case, 6. so that, 7. as, 8. before, 9. because, 10. when
Challenge: answers may vary

Page 7
Practice: 1. bi, 2. sub, 3. aero, 4. im 5. in, 6. ir, 7. tri, 8. il, 9. pre, 10. de, 11. mis, 12. re, 13. centi, 14. anti, 15. ex
Challenge: 1. baby, 2. nasty, 3. beauty, 4. quarrel, 5. shine, 6. operate, 7. knife, 8. microscope, 9. burgle, 10. mystery, 11. attend, 12. excite

Page 8
Practice: 2. was driven (P), 3. wrote (A), 4. listened (A), 5. was won (P), 6. was chopped (P), 7. ran (A), 8. was blown (P), 9. bought (A), 10. crashed (A), 11. was scored (P), 12. chased (A)
Challenge:
2. A porter carried my luggage.
3. The cat chased the mouse.
4. The relay team won the gold medal.
5. The boy picked up the coin.
6. The girl broke the window.
7. Sam dropped the glass.
8. The horse ate the carrot.
9. The thief stole all the keys.
10. Ben's aunt hugged him.

Page 9
Practice: 1. Scarlet, 2. bracket, 3. bouquet, 4. sachet, 5. trumpet, 6. duvet, 7. cabaret, 8. ballet, 9. banquet, 10. blanket, 11. buffet, 12. ricochet
Challenge: 1. Italy, 2. Holland, 3. France, 4. Australia, 5. China, 6. America, 7. India, 8. Jamaica

Page 10
Practice: 2. separate, 3. favourite, 4. bicycle, 5. conscience, 6. piece, 7. young, 8. believe, 9. miserable, 10. weight
Challenge: answers may vary

Page 11
Practice:
1. The man asked, "Is it raining?"
2. "I've lost my pen," Rohan shouted.
3. The burglar whispered, "Someone's coming!"
4. "Where's my bag?" Mrs Shah asked.
5. You will need a pen, a ruler and some paper.
6. The noise, a loud banging noise, was awful.
7. The children's clothes were on the floor.
8. "What a lovely surprise!" the teacher said.
9. "Pass the salt, please," Sam's dad asked.
10. The boy's coat was torn.

Challenge: Danger? No. Swimming allowed!

Page 12
Practice: 2. scribble, describe, 3. vision, evident, 4. pedal, pedestrian, 5. grateful, congratulate, 6. spectator, spectacles, 7. liberty, liberal, 8. city, civilian
Challenge: answers may vary

Page 13
Practice:
1. The children began to shout when the teacher left the room.
2. Last night I read a good book when I went to bed.
3. Alexander Bell was the inventor who invented the telephone.
4. I visited Athens which is in Greece.
5. I collect stamps because they are so colourful.
6. Samuel Pepys lived in London during the Great Fire in 1666.

Challenge: answers may vary

Page 14
Practice: 1. cooks, 2. speed, 3. served, 4. never, 5. well, 6. clean, 7. nine, 8. one, 9. worm, 10. birds
Challenge:
1. has a silver lining.
2. make most noise.
3. in one basket.
4. run deep.
5. deserves another.
6. gathers no moss.
7. think alike but fools seldom differ.
8. into the fire.

Page 15
Practice: 2. umbrella, 3. confident, 4. electric, 5. infected, 6. introduce, 7. chatterbox, 8. hospital, 9. restlessness, 10. remember, 11. different, 12. January, 13. attention, 14. uniform, 15. conductor
Challenge: 2. November, 3. proposal, 4. helplessly, helpfully, 5. adventure, 6. lemonade, 7.excellent, 8. disaster, 9. confident, 10. expensive, extensive

Page 16
Practice: 2. Beautiful, 3. Cork, 4. Dangerous, 5. Expensive, 6. Ford, 7. Glance, 8. Hexagon, 9. Icicle, 10. Jeer, 11. Knife, 12. Lance, 13. Mask, 14. Narrow, 15. Octopus , 16. Peaceful, 17. Quay, 18. Recent, 19. Scarce, 20. Till, 21. Unite, 22. Vague, 23. Witty, 24. Xmas, 25. Yacht, 26. Zoom
Challenge: 2. reservoir, 3. parliament, 4. government, 5. delicious, 6. disappear, 7. somersault, 8. altogether,9. scissors, 10. kangaroo

Page 17
Practice: 2. believe, 3. brief, 4. chief, 5. field, 6. shield, 7. piece, 8. siege, 9. babies, 10. copies, 11. ceiling, 12. receive, 13. deceive, 14. perceive, 15. conceit
Challenge: 1. priest, 2. mischief, 3. deceit, 4. relief, 5. ceiling, 6. niece, 7. shriek, 8. sieve, 9. conceited, 10. yield, 11. receive, 12. fierce